Birds of the Yorkshire Coast

by

Richard Vaughan

Cover picture: Purple sandpiper at Filey Brigg

HENDON PUBLISHING, NELSON, LANCASHIRE

First published in Great Britain 1974
by Hendon Publishing Co., Ltd.,
Hendon Mill,
Nelson,
Lancashire.

Hardback edition: ISBN 0 902907 54 9
Softback edition: ISBN 0 902907 55 7

Printed in Great Britain by
Turner & Earnshaw Ltd.,
Bread Street,
Burnley,
Lancashire.

Contents

Introduction

This booklet needs little by way of introduction. Its aim is to present a portrait of the bird life of Yorkshire's coast in photographs, every one of which has been taken in Yorkshire at the place indicated or under discussion. The great majority of species commonly occurring are represented here; those that are not, the shelduck, scoter and sand martin perhaps the most conspicuous among them, are omitted because I have not photographed them on the Yorkshire coast. None of the photographs reproduced here have been published before.

The Yorkshire coast comprises in essence two large muddy estuaries situated at either end of it, the Tees and the Humber; a series of cliffs where the North Yorkshire Moors and the Wolds meet the sea; and the long low clay cliff of Holderness, extending southwards from Bridlington to Kilnsea and Spurn Point. Birds tend to be concentrated at certain points, and this is reflected in the distribution of photographs in this book. By far the largest and finest concentration of birds in summer occurs on the incomparable chalk cliffs of Bempton and Flamborough. In winter, on the other hand, most birds are seen at Teesmouth and Spurn, at Filey Brigg, and occasionally in the harbours at Whitby, Scarborough or Bridlington.

For assistance in the preparation of this book I am particularly indebted to my wife Margaret, who helped me take many of the photographs and who herself took the photograph on page 12, and to my children. I thank also the many bird watchers who have encouraged and helped me in one way or another, in particular Henry Bunce and Alan Credland.

Teesmouth

The estuary of the River Tees separates Yorkshire from Durham in the north just as the Humber formed the boundary between Yorkshire and Lincolnshire in the south. These two estuaries at the two extremes of the Yorkshire coast provide its only substantial areas of tidal mudflat.

Teesmouth has been a well-known haunt of migrating and wintering birds ever since the author of *The Birds of Yorkshire,* Thomas Nelson, watched it regularly at the end of the nineteenth century. Industrial Development was even at that time encroaching on marsh and mudflat; since then a great deal of reclamation and building has further restricted the areas available for birds. Docks, chemical factories and oil refineries are scarcely even suitable for sparrows. To reach the best area for birds on the Yorkshire side of the Tees you have practically to drive through a steel works, blandly disregarding a horrifying battery of frighteningly prohibitory notices. Eventually you reach the South Gare peninsula, which culminates in a massive breakwater or mole built of huge slabs of concrete with a coastguard tower and lighthouse perched on it. It looks for all the world like some old fashioned ship lurching out to sea. From here, on one side, a fine beach of smooth yellow sand extends eastwards to Coatham; on the other side ships move ceaselessly in and out of the estuary against a background of pylons, cooling towers, smoking chimneys, high steel fences, pipes belching steam, and tall cranes. But do not imagine that the unspoilt natural beauty of Coatham sands steals all the limelight. On a calm September night, when curlews and whimbrels call overhead, even the shimmer of the harvest moon on the sea by Redcar will not for long keep one's admiring attention from the myriad coloured lights of the Teesside works; the red and white lights twinkling in the water; the moving lights of ships; and the pale calm waters fringed by rocks where oystercatchers and other waders feed and call in the darkness.

Teesmouth's surviving marshes, its mud, its mole-protected waters, offer refuge and food through the winter to seagulls of several species. Here flights of teal and wigeon and many other ducks congregate to feed. Above all, this is a place for waders. Several hundred bar-tailed godwits have been counted on Bran Sands in January. Oystercatchers feed on the rocks at South Gare and spend the high-tide period on Coatham sands, where I have counted over 350 sanderlings, also roosting at high tide. Teesmouth is a favourite locality, too, for cormorants and for many other seabirds. In August and September migrating terns and skuas gather in the mouth of the estuary and may be admirably observed from the South Gare breakwater. Many rarities have been seen here. For example on 14 and 15 August 1971, all the four species of skua recorded in the British Isles were seen from the breakwater, and the same year produced a Sabine's gull and sooty shearwaters at the same place. No wonder that, in spite of the threat of more reclamation and more industry, bird watchers are attracted here in numbers and Teesmouth has its own bird club with a quarterly bird report.

This kittiwake was photographed on 12 September 1973, on the South Gare breakwater. The smoky patch behind the bird's eye shows that it is in winter plumage.

Skuas at South Gare. Above: an Arctic skua flies past low over the murky water of the Tees against a backcloth of industry. Also visible is an adult kittiwake in flight. Left: the skuas find sustenance while on migration by chasing terns and taking their food. Here an Arctic skua is about to seize a small fish from a common tern. The bird behind the tern is a juvenile herring gull.

The author photographing a juvenile kittiwake on the South Gare breakwater, Teesmouth. For some reason both young and old kittiwakes frequenting this breakwater in September 1973, were exceptionally tame and could be approached to within a few feet.

Favourite haunt of sanderlings on the Yorkshire coast—Coatham sands, near Redcar.
These birds, superbly camouflaged among the shingle and boulders, are resting during the
high-tide period.

Whitby and Robin Hood's Bay

From Saltburn south-eastwards to Whitby and beyond a magnificent range of variously coloured cliffs fringes the North Sea. Some of the towns and villages that nestle along this shore in sheltered valleys and creeks have become noted beauty spots: Staithes and Runswick Bay, as well as Whitby itself and Robin Hood's Bay. Although scenically superb, and mostly within the boundaries of the North Yorkshire Moors National Park, this stretch of coastline is ornithologically nonedescript. Whitby harbour is an exception, for in winter it offers welcome shelter to stormbound seabirds and sea ducks, divers and grebes may be seen there at such times. In summer the cliffs hereabouts hold breeding birds such as fulmars and herring gulls, and there are flourishing colonies of kittiwakes and cormorants, for example at Huntcliff near Saltburn, where oystercatchers, redshanks and turnstones feed on the flat seaweed-covered rocks called Scars.

The ornithological speciality of this part of Yorkshire's coast are the herring gull colonies on houses at Whitby and Robin Hood's Bay. It is apparently only in the last thirty years or so that gulls have taken to nesting on buildings. In Yorkshire the habit was first noted in the Second World War at Bridlington, for in the years when the North Pier of the harbour there was closed to the public, herring gulls nested on it. Then, in 1947, gulls were found nesting on houses at Robin Hood's Bay and Staithes. Meanwhile colonies of herring gulls nesting in towns had been established elsewhere, at Newquay, Cornwall, about 1926 and at Dover in 1936. A survey carried out in 1969-70 showed that well over a thousand pairs of gulls were at that time nesting on buildings in Britain: in the summer of 1970 I counted forty-two pairs on roofs and chimneys at Whitby, all with occupied nests.

A large part of the charm of places like Staithes and Robin Hood's Bay lies in their herring gulls, which are resident throughout the year. The birds are beautiful in themselves and become very tame and approachable so that they can be seen to better advantage than most other wild birds. Their behaviour is quite fascinating, especially as the breeding season approaches and the gulls are beginning their courtship. But most attractive of all are their superb melodious calls, which resound incessantly summer and winter, loud and clear over the narrow streets of these picturesque Yorkshire fishing villages.

Herring gulls on the roofs and chimneys at Whitby. The birds shown here are not at their nests but have gathered in a neutral non-territorial assembly area for which the name 'club' has been used.

The herring gull family pictured above has taken up residence on the roof of a church at Robin Hood's Bay. Other places noted for their roof or chimney-nesting gulls are Whitby and Dover.

18

A well-grown young herring gull with its parent on a roof at Robin Hood's Bay in July 1970. Among the human residents, these birds have their friends and enemies, but for most visitors they add considerably to the charm and interest of this famous Yorkshire beauty spot.

Some householders in Robin Hood's Bay have erected anti-gull devices on their chimneys. The herring gull pictured above, though prevented from building a nest, has nonetheless found a convenient perching and resting place. At Scarborough the gulls' attempts to breed have been discouraged by shooting.

Filey Brigg

This natural breakwater of sloping slabs of rock juts seawards from the clay-capped headland of Carr Naze on the northern shore of Filey Bay. At high tide it is often covered by the sea; at low tide in calm weather one can walk out half a mile or so dry shod. No birds nest on its sea-washed rocks and in summer, usually crowded with people, it is deserted by birds. But throughout the autumn, winter and spring it is the finest place for the birdwatcher anywhere on the Yorkshire coast - always excepting Spurn. Indeed its astonishing and ever lengthening list of rarities makes it one of the very best spots in Britain for seeing unusual seabirds. Moreover, the large number of photographs taken there which are reproduced in this book is excellent evidence of its suitability for watching and photographing the commoner species, many of which can be seen there more easily and more frequently than anywhere else.

The barnacle and mussel encrusted rocks of the Brigg make it an excellent feeding ground for wading birds at low tide. Oystercatchers, knots, dunlins, purple sandpipers and turnstones are nearly always to be found. These and other waders as well as gulls and cormorants use the Brigg as a resting and roosting place, especially at high tide. But the Brigg is also admirably placed for watching the passage of seabirds, above all in spring and autumn, when divers, shearwaters, skuas, gannets and duck of many species can be seen at sea. In the autumn, too, there can be few better places than the Brigg for watching that always exciting phenomenon, the visible migration of land birds. For here you may stand on a November afternoon and actually see blackbirds, redwings and other birds flying in from the sea to make their first landfall after crossing the North Sea from Scandinavia.

Filey is too small to boast a bird club of its own, but few interesting birds passing or visiting the Brigg are missed by that indefatigable and hawk-eyed Scarborough ornithologist, Ron Appleby.

Purple sandpipers and other waders are often forced to take sudden flight as sheets of churning foam rush over the flat rocks on which they love to feed near the end of Filey Brigg. On this occasion the photographer too was forced to beat a hasty retreat.

Skuas are seen along the Yorkshire coast every autumn on their way south from their northern breeding grounds. This juvenile Arctic skua was resting on Filey Brigg on 8 September 1970.

A few long-tailed ducks visit Filey Brigg in winter from their Scandinavian summer quarters. The handsome drakes in winter plumage with their white heads and long tails are very distinctive. These birds sometimes feed close inshore in the bay.

A pair of long-tailed ducks feeding in Filey Bay close to the Brigg. These birds feed by diving and on the left the pair have been caught by the camera diving simultaneously.

The eiders which feed off Filey Brigg and in Filey Bay during the winter months are seldom seen out of the water. This young drake in pied plumage, transitional between the juvenile brown and the striking black and white of the adult male, was photographed on 31 January 1970.

The kittiwakes which crowd onto Filey Brigg in the late summer and early autumn are often quite tame. Except at times and places like this, these birds can seldom be photographed away from their breeding cliffs, for they spend most of the rest of the year at sea. This photograph was taken in mid-September 1968, when there was a preponderance of adult birds among the large numbers of kittiwakes present on the Brigg.

The herring gulls of Filey depend in large measure for their livelihood on the abundant supplies of fish offal which are thrown overboard from the fishing cobles as they return to the landing place after a successful trip. In these illustrations the boats and their attendant birds, in reality far out in Filey Bay, are brought into apparent proximity by a powerful telephoto lens: above, against the background of Filey Brigg as seen from the coble landing at Filey; and opposite, viewed from the Brigg itself, with the sea reflecting the light of the afternoon sun, while in the distance the towering cliffs of Bempton and Speeton, dark because in shadow, take the place of sky.

30

One of the rarer winter visitors to the Yorkshire coast is the glaucous gull, which can be distinguished at once from the commoner species of gull by the complete absence of any black at the tips of its wings. This immature bird was photographed as it sat on the beach at Filey on 2 January 1968. In Iceland, which is the glaucous gull's nearest breeding place to Britain, it interbreeds with the herring gull.

A common tern in flight over Filey Brigg. Thousands of these graceful birds pass down the Yorkshire coast every autumn on their way to winter quarters in the south from their breeding colonies, the nearest of which to Yorkshire are those on the Farne Islands.

Filey Brigg often serves as a refuge, too often unfortunately the last refuge, for birds whose plumage has been damaged by oil at sea. These two badly oiled guillemots were photographed on 17 September 1968, after a particularly bad incident.

A shag rests sitting bolt up-right on a rock near the end of the Brigg.

A shag feeding. The tremendous force of the shag's plunge brings the whole of its body momentarily clear of the water (left). The incandescent dots and circles are a characteristic effect of the mirror lens used for both these photographs, which invariably renders the sparkle of reflected sunlight on water in this way. This bird was photographed from Filey Brigg in March.

Purple sandpipers, which nest in the Scandinavian highlands and visit British shores only in winter, can always be found at that season on the Brigg. Water swirls round a group of these birds photographed on 12 November 1967, when they had assembled together before starting their high-tide sleep.

A purple sandpiper at Filey Brigg bathes in the sea. It has lowered itself partly into the water and is shaking its tail end vigorously to and fro.

Portrait of a purple sandpiper, photographed on Filey Brigg in September, 1973.

A bar-tailed godwit photographed as it waded feeding in Filey Bay on 8 September, 1970. This wader is common on passage and in the winter in the Tees and Humber but is not so often seen along the rest of the Yorkshire coast. The first birds moving south appear in late July.

Many birds use Filey Brigg
a resting or roosting plac
especially at high tide. Here
group of knots, with on
turnstone, are sleeping awa
the high-tide period when the
feeding grounds are unde
water.

Crowding along the shore line, nervous and ready for instant flight, these knots were photographed on 26 January 1968, when over fifty were present on the Brigg; the wintering population is usually a good deal smaller than this.

The knot is one of those waders that occasionally permits close approach with a camera.
This bird was one of several feeding at the end of Filey Brigg in September 1973.

A little stint photographed on the Brigg on 8 September 1970. This tiny sparrow-sized wader is an irregular passage visitor only to the Yorkshire coast.

Filey Brigg's only truly resident species, the aptly-named rock pipit, runs on the smooth tide-worn rocks like a wagtail, and supplements its winter diet with crumbs left by anglers and bird watchers.

Bempton and Flamborough

Between Reighton Gap and Sewerby or, less exactly, between Filey and Bridlington, vertical white chalk cliffs, capped with clay of varying thickness, and rising in places straight from the sea, afford nesting places secure from animal predators for thousands of sea birds. On these cliffs, which vary in height from about 200 to over 400 feet, is England's largest kittiwake colony, Britain's only mainland gannet colony, and Yorkshire's only nesting colony of shags. Besides the kittiwakes, one other species of gull is a very numerous breeder here, the herring gull; while great black-backed gulls spend the summer below the cliffs and prey on the breeding birds. Three species of auk nest here in thousands: the guillemot, razorbill and puffin; and one petrel, the fulmar, is common. Several species of land bird also nest in or on these cliffs: house and tree sparrows, starlings, jackdaws, house martins; not to mention more or less wild rock doves.

From the village of Bempton a narrow straight road leads to a rough but adequate grassy cliff-top car park. A visit here on a fine day in summer is an unforgettable experience. Brilliant white against the dark blue sea far below, thousands of kittiwakes wheel and cry, sending up a confused but sweet-sounding jumble of 'kittiwaak' calls. Puffins, razorbills and guillemots zoom to and fro with their bullet-shaped bodies and short stubby whirring wings, while the fulmars glide incessantly along the cliff top, banking almost vertically as they turn to come back and, so it seems, take a second look at the intruder. In the excitement of watching the birds swarming in the air, one forgets the myriads more on the ledges, visible from many a vantage point on the cliff top to which the visitor is led by well-worn tracks through the long grass, nettles and other luxuriant vegetation. A fetid, by not altogether unpleasant smell assails the nostrils as one looks over the cliffs. Everywhere there are kittiwakes, some with nests high up near the top, others far down below almost washed by sea spray. So enthralling is it to watch so many birds in such ideal conditions that one scarcely notices the passage of time. One can expect to be late returning home from a visit to Bempton.

The gannets of Bempton. The breeding gannets occupy the diagonal ledge one-third way down the cliff shown here, which drops 400 feet sheer into the sea.

The gannets' love-making a
Bempton. The male seizes th
female firmly with his powe
ful bill by the back of he
neck before mounting he
(right). This pair has not ye
built its nest though a star
has been made by gatherin
some seaweed for the purpose

This general view of the main part of the gannet colony was taken on 23 June, 1973, when some of the chicks were well feathered. It is the upper part of this section of the colony which is seen opposite enlarged, but five years earlier

A close-up of the gannets of Bempton. These fine birds only began to nest in Yorkshire in or shortly before 1937, forming Britain's only mainland gannet colony. Now over twenty pairs nest annually and in July 1973 at least 70 adult birds were present. Shown here is the most crowded part of the gannet's main ledge, on 9 July 1968.

Herring gulls at Flamborough. This pair were photographed copulating on one of the bare rounded clay slopes above the chalk cliffs near the coastguard station. The male calls repeatedly while mounting the female.

Herring gulls at Flamborough. Courtship feeding (1): The male (right) is about to regurgitate food for the female: note the lump in his throat.

Herring gulls at Flamborough. Courtship feeding (2): The male's regurgitated food drops to the ground and the female (left) begins to eat it.

Herring gulls at Flamborough. Courtship feeding (3): The female, on left, eagerly swallows the food disgorged by her mate. This ritual feeding is probably essential for the female, to enable her to lay her clutch of three large eggs.

57

Herring gulls with chicks at Flamborough. Above: while the female stands guard the three chicks, having left their nest (centre), respond to her alarm notes by crouching in a rock crevice where their protective colouring makes them hard to see. Left: two chicks, only a few days old, peep out from under their parent's wing.

In May the kittiwakes gather in the fields and in and around the cliff-top ponds at Bempton to collect nest material (above). Nest-building is very much a communal activity and at times a constant stream of birds carrying nest material in their beaks flies from the collecting grounds to the breeding cliffs (left).

The hordes of breeding kittiwakes at Bempton and Flamborough leave the cliffs and fly inland a few hundred yards for two reasons only: to collect nest material and to drink or bathe in fresh water. Below: some thirsty birds are visiting a pool above the cliffs at Flamborough. Left: kittiwakes in May collecting water weed and grass from a cliff-top pond at Bempton in order to make their nests.

When they first return to their breeding colony in March, kittiwakes spend most of their time sleeping, preening themselves, or just standing on the remains of their last years' nests. This is one of the countless Flamborough nesting pairs.

e kittiwake's greeting cere-
ny, here seen performed
ly in the season before
sts have been built or re-
ilt. Both birds call loudly
ttiwaak'and bow their heads
and down rhythmically.

66   Razorbills on the sea below their breeding cliffs at Flamborough.

An assembly of guillemots below the breeding cliffs at Flamborough; this rock is covered by the sea at high tide.

This razorbill was photographed as it shot past the author while he stood on the cliff-top at Bempton. The beautiful streamlining of its body is particularly in evidence when a bird is gliding.

Razorbills often sit about near
he tops of the cliffs at Bem-
ton and can sometimes be
pproached quite closely. Even
o, this bird had to be photo-
raphed with a 1000mm lens.

Puffins are sociable birds and love to congregate in groups. This ledge at Flamborough is a favourite gathering place of these charming birds.

eding guillemots at Petrel
le, near the coastguard
ion, Flamborough. This was
 main species to suffer
m the activities of the
nbers at Bempton, who
d to collect thousands of
s annually.

By no means all the birds of the Yorkshire coast are sea-birds. Jackdaws breed commonly at Flamborough and Bempton and prey on the kittiwakes, robbing them of their eggs. This juvenile jackdaw was photographed at Flamborough on 5 July 1970.

In March, when many of the Flamborough kittiwakes' nests are still untenanted, the jackdaws squabble for the few available holes in the chalk cliffs. The right-hand bird of those in this photograph repeatedly attacked the pair in possession of the hole, sometimes bringing its mate along with it.

The house martin is another non sea-bird which nests commonly on the cliffs at Flamborough.
They tuck their mud-built nests under an overhang to protect them from the weather.

Sewerby and Bridlington

Near Sewerby the chalk cliffs of Flamborough come to an end, giving place to clay. A few pairs of fulmars nest here, but otherwise it is the wintering birds which make this shore of ornithological interest. On the broad flat chalk beach up to a hundred crows regularly feed, among them a few hooded crows, and an important winter population of waders is to be found, including redshanks, dunlins, turnstones and ringed plovers. On the sea, eiders, scoters and other sea ducks sometimes assemble or feed, and there are always gulls to be seen. A walk here in winter along the cliff top to the Danes Dike and back by the beach is strongly recommended.

At Bridlington it is the harbour which is the centre of attraction for birds. Redshanks and other waders feed on its mud at low tide, and cormorants, grebes and sea ducks seek refuge in it from time to time, especially in stormy winter weather. Just south of the harbour's south wall a few purple sandpipers can often be seen feeding on the seaweed covered rocks at low tide; eiders are sometimes seen here in winter; and up to fifty sanderlings feed on the sands. Four species of gull can be seen together on the beach at Bridlington in winter: great black-backed, herring, common and black-headed.

A rare visitor from Scandinavia, a red-necked grebe which spent several weeks at Bridlington in the winter of 1970-71 in company with another bird of its species. This grebe has been known to spend over a minute under water while diving for the small fish it feeds on. Denmark is the nearest breeding place to England.

A cormorant photographed in autumn in Bridlington Harbour. It has just surfaced from a dive and still has droplets of water on its back. Most dives last half a minute or less, but exceptionally a cormorant has been recorded staying under water for over a minute.

The sands south of the harbour at Bridlington are a favourite place for sanderling in winter. One January I managed to approach close to these usually wary little waders at high tide when they were feeding and resting close to the promenade. A common coastal and estuarine winter visitor in England, the sanderling's nearest breeding grounds are in Greenland and Spitzbergen.

Not far from Bridlington, Hornsea Mere, because of its proximity to the sea, acts as a refuge for many seabirds. Cormorants, for example, are to be seen there throughout the year, and every autumn in recent years the rather uncommon little gull has been present there in small numbers. This bird occurs at Spurn and elsewhere on the Yorkshire coast. Here the adult's winter plumage may be compared with the very striking black-and-white plumage of the young 'bird of the year'. The little gull is the world's smallest gull; it breeds just across the North Sea in Denmark.

Eiders diving for weed at Bridlington in January 1974. They allowed me to photograph them at close quarters from the sea wall at high tide. Note the way the bird in the background on the opposite page uses its wings at the start of its dive.

The fulmar petrel was first recorded breeding in Yorkshire in 1922 at Bempton. Since then it has become a common breeder all along the cliffs as far south as Sewerby where this photograph was taken. These birds were paying a December visit to their breeding cliffs.

Spurn and the Humber

Britain's third bird observatory was established at Spurn in 1945 for the study and ringing of birds on migration. Spurn is a long, low, narrow sandy peninsula which curves southwestwards across the mouth of the Humber from the northern shore by Kilnsea. Near its tip wartime defences and encampments have almost obliterated the natural landscape of dunes and sea buckthorn scrub. Room has been found here, too, for a lifeboat and a row of cottages for its crew, for whom a tiny chapel has been provided among the old nissen huts, watch towers and gun emplacements. Migrant wheatears perch on the wall of what was once the parade ground. Tree sparrows nest in nest boxes or in holes in buildings and walls. The wire netting trap, carefully sited in an area of scrub near the point, is worked regularly and successfully and the birds caught there ringed. The observatory buildings, Warden's cottage, common room, dormitories for visiting bird watchers, are situated near the northern end of the peninsula, where there is another trap and a commodious hut for watching birds passing at sea. Spurn Bird Observatory does things in style. Its annual report, written and produced by the Warden, Barry Spence, is a model of its kind: accurate, succinct, informative and, most importantly, punctual, for it invariably appears within a few months of the end of each year. The Yorkshire Naturalists' Trust owns Spurn Peninsula; the Yorkshire Naturalists' Union runs the Spurn Bird Observatory.

Spurn Point is one of the most famous places in Britain for rare birds. Its tip marked the southern end of the coast of Yorkshire, but the Humber estuary, reaching inland to Goole, cannot be left out of account. On the northern shore, Cherry Cob Sands and Brough Haven are perhaps the best known places for seeing waders at high tide. Both spots can boast quite long lists of rarities. On the Humber mud the commonest winter wader is the dunlin but the mud also supports large numbers of curlews, redshanks and other waders. Duck too are often abundant, especially shelducks, mallard and wigeon. At the upper end of the Humber the Humber Wildfowl Refuge was established to protect the wintering flock of pink-footed geese, but this fine bird has become much rarer in this area in recent years.

Migration at Spurn. Scarcely a bird of the coast? But the wheatear is in fact seen commonly on migration all along the Yorkshire coast. This one was perched on the Parade Ground wall at Spurn on 18 September 1969.

This tree sparrow is about
squeeze itself into a one-i
diameter hole in the concr
wall which surrounds the
mer parade ground at Sp
Point, in order to feed
young. It carries a ring on
left leg, almost certainly pla
there by the Warden of Spu
Mr. Barry Spence, when it
a nestling, perhaps in one
the nest boxes which h
been put up there for th
and other birds. The tree s
rows at Spurn Point belong
a mixed house sparrow a
tree sparrow colony, but
holes in the parade grou
wall are too small for
house sparrows to use.
Flamborough and Bemp
tree sparrows breed in h
near the top of the cliffs.

Along much of the Yorkshire coast the carrion crow is a common scavenger on the beach. This one was photographed at Spurn while it cawed repeatedly. At Sewerby there are often upwards of a hundred crows feeding on the shore in winter, with hooded crows among them.

Waders photographed at Chalk Bank, Spurn, as they flew past the author's hide. Left: a flock of oystercatchers heads across to the Lincolnshire shore of the Humber. Above: a group of turnstones in flight low over the sand display their wing patterns. The oystercatchers, photographed in January, show the white neck spots of their winter plumage. Two of the turnstones above are moulting their wing feathers — they were photographed in September.

Common gulls in winter over the Humber at Hull. These birds gather at the Victoria Pier, Hull and at New Holland, and follow the Humber Ferries to and fro, taking scraps of bread thrown to them. The common gull is a regular but not very abundant winter visitor to the Humber; it does not breed in Yorkshire.